hive mind

medusa collective

BookLeaf Publishing

India | USA | UK

Presentation by *BookLeaf Publishing*

Web: www.bookleafpub.com

E-mail: info@bookleafpub.com

ISBN: 9789360940546

First edition 2024

An Invocation of My Muse

Of the future, the never-ending past,
Of pleasure indistinguishable from pain,
Gashes on tongues,
Gashes between legs,
Speak, O Muse, with bloodstained lips
of bloodless bodies
with hearts too big for our cold, cruel world!

Speak, O Muse, with hair like crows and snakes;
Unravel our serpent souls,
Release me from the dread,
Teeth marks on tongues,
Teeth marks between legs,
The wariness that lives forever in our cold bones!

Hold my feverish head, O Mother,
while my body rots at your feet,
set me free so that I may Speak, O Muse,

With a voice like thunder and choruses of children,
Speak-- scream!-- though They may only hear
when the world goes silent.

The Silver Charm

This story has no ending, and it begins with a lamb,
a mother with twin rivers that fall from her eyes
to save a magical wizard child.

Swaddled in a basket, safe and dry,
the magical child floats down the stream
with a home, a necklace, of generational silver,
crying, screaming, from the heat of the flames that paint the
sky,
the tree branches that burn and fall, hissing
in the turbulent water that rocks the magical child to sleep.

The magical child is allowed to grow.
The magical child is allowed to learn, to love,
to hate the fire, the fire-bringers that scorch silver
and the homes of many others.

The magical child is allowed to save the world.
The magical child is allowed to grow old, to love,
to love the fire, that warms stoves and brings heat
to the homes of those that have been saved.

This story has no ending, but it always begins with a lamb,
and a home, burnt by evil
with a child of magic, who saves
a world's worth of homes.

They never know, and are never told,
of the sacrificial lamb that was never expected to live,
never destined to be safe.

Phantasmagoria

I wait for the day that the purpose of life
is more than survival, than learning to sit still
amidst constant, dizzying, eternal motion
Than searching for a satisfaction that fights to be
released
or drips between cracks in fingers like water
returning to the pool, to the air, falling back to the
earth.

I search for identity in a world ruled by distinction
Where you are only when you are not, or you are
more
or you are less, but you are never equal
and you are never alone, for then, you would cease to
exist.

To trust in the existence of something better
is to be capable of fathoming something more
than what is tangible, what is real,
and what has always been.
An element yet to be discovered,
a principle of life governed by the laws
of a science that humanity has no desire to discover.

Last Night

Last night, I fell in love, and the day after,
I return to the Earth, to the passage of time,
to the space marked clearly, between sunrise and
sunset.

Last night, I broke my own heart.
I learned I break before I am broken.
And the sunrise illuminates the life in front of me
I have yet to plan. There are words I have yet to read,
yet to say, and there is a need to know how
and when to say them.

Last night, I returned to myself.
I sat in the quiet, when time did not exist
yet continued moving forward.
And when the sunlight comes, I shield my eyes on
my drive.
I drive, and I drive, I work, then drive again,
I go and I come, then I eat, I clean. I plan,
and I create, I contribute, then
I find more to be done.

Saltwater baby

5

I turn a year older at the beach, where life imitates art,
where I finally welcome the saltwater that burns my eyes.

I don't go too far, not into the water,
not away from home,
not when I hold my tongue,
nor beyond the memories behind my eyes before I fall
asleep.

There is a grain of sand for my every wish
and for every path I have not taken,
where hermit crabs shuffle along, looking for bigger shells.

I wake up early for every sunrise
to stare at the molten copper rising from the ocean,
but never find any greater meaning.

The only evidence of a vacation for a troubled mind
are the tan lines that will eventually fade.

14, February

6

Like the flowers that lose their petals,
velvet curtains pulling apart to fall
ash to ashes
petals to dust,
the Earth will soon consume me,
mud bubbling at my ankles, grass rising between toes,
in a heaving breath, waiting to take me deep
into Her lungs.

Press me into the pages of your book
where She can take me no more,
where you can run your fingers over my velvet
and remember when I was younger
and alive.

The Companion

The bloodshot eye that watches me tonight
has no need for corners, or places to hide.
It floats above my bed with no need for limbs
and has no mouth to wish me goodnight.
Sometimes it cries, and I wipe its tears,
but it has no hands, so it does not wipe mine.
My chest swells with panic when the eye grows in
size;
I'm unsure if it will hurt me, how, or why,
with no limbs, no mouth, only spider leg lashes
that cast shadows like claw marks on skin.

I do not know when it was born,
or what would give birth to such a thing.
I do not know if it was ever loved,
or if love is all it wants from me.

Bottle Redhead

8

You do not know me. I do not exist.
And to know me is to know a world of pain
and medicine that pushes you deeper into sickness.

You do not see me. I do not exist.
And to see me is to see expectations unmet
and a thousand lives that never lived.

You can never know what does not know itself,
what yearns to be left unknown.
You can never see what the mirror does not reflect,
what yearns to change, deceive.

Metamorphosis

9

I dream of chapped lips and cranberry kisses
and the days when I could not recognize the smell of blood.
To keep track of time, I count the inches of my hair
left undamaged by earlier attempts at playing God.

There have always been words lingering between the lines,
long before rage replaced my brick wall despair.
They call out to me now like modern prophecies.
I am cursed- indeed I am blessed!- to be driven mad from
Revelation!

TUNNEL VISION

Yearning has been my superstition
when looking at you has only made you disappear.

I see stars and speak your name, I make friendship
bracelets
from my gaze and my heart which are hard and pink
like rose quartz

but I have supermassive black holes for eyes
that suck in space and steal your light

that press you to my dense core as I collapse
on myself and rip you to ribbons

all the hearts I've buried have had short lives

but the rot of death is never stagnant

it is never buried.

"Situationship"

I love you like a lamb loves slaughter,
like a virgin waiting blissfully to be sacrificed-
I need you, need to breathe you like carbon monoxide,
need to feel your heat, like alcohol burning my insides
as I lay frostbitten in soft, unforgiving snow

in spite of sense and rationality,
searching for solace, succumbing to an inevitable end.

a woman. scorned.

12

At times she cannot bear to hear laughter
so hearty and full, breaking apart and spilling
like blood from an engorged mosquito between palms.

At times she is reminded of the eternally burning sun,
the source of all nature, a bringer of life
and how, regardless, every sunflower eventually wilts
as if its devotion was never enough.

Illusion of Reciprocity

13

It is a sweet, bubbling chirp, that wafts through a spring
breeze
that draws the bird from its perch in the trees
with a promise of companionship in
the way of nature, when nature is as it should be.
It is a seduction that draws the bird to commence
a search for the possibility of a forever,
a chirp that promises no solitude until there is death,
where until there is death, there will only be more life.

It is a sweet, bubbling chirp that wafts through the spring
breeze
from the lips of the man who wants only to see
what his sound shall bring, if there is anything that will
listen
to the language he speaks but does not understand.
He does not know why the bird does not rejoice
at the sight of him, why it does not sing for him,
and why it does not applaud his clever mimicry
when he has so clearly proven that nature is what he
chooses
that it will be, which the bird is clearly
not human enough to understand.

Symbiosis

14

There is something I feel when my cat asks for affection,
her little face splitting open to a cavern of fangs
with the sound of a newborn, spanked fresh from the
womb.
I feel it again tonight, when my drive comes to a violent
halt
for glowing eyes that could not meet mine past the metal
and glass;
When the deer crosses the beams of my headlight and I
patiently wait,
and thank it for trusting me
in spite of my humanity.

Choose your own adventure

This forest teems with life, but its eyes are jaundiced,
its birds fly through smoke and scream songs of loss.
Its crumbling temples hold well-worn scrolls that
speak of potions
and the eyes speak of dark pasts, dark futures, and the
darker intentions
of the powers of false gods that seek to destroy your
home.
(Offer your condolences, as you cannot fight a higher
power - stanza 2)
(Read from the knowledge of the scrolls, you may
find a way - stanza 3)

Your decision does not seem to faze the eyes.
They blink slowly, knowingly, but never close for
long.
You plug your ears at the birds that once screamed,
the birds that once flew, and they succumb to the
smoke.
They drop like flies, and you feed from their
cancerous meat;
You drink from rivers of polluted, bloodied sludge
that pass through your body like the cement that
petrifies the trees.
Your eyes see it all, but the forest does not let you
die.
Your eyes watch the cruelty that builds death upon
life,

pouring cement on your brethren,
that taunts your choice in the face of destruction.
You are not allowed to die, so you must always
watch,
for even after you attempt to enter the darkness,
the dying forest does not let you die.
The eyes you gouge out live to blink endlessly at
passersby.
(You were not the first to refuse the forest - stanza 4)

The papers glow with magic and hope
telling tales of birds that sing cures, and plants that
give life.
But burning skies are not home to birds that sing,
and polluted rivers do not and cannot grow plants.
Magic and hope feed your hungry ambition, but not
your hungry mouth;
You listen for answers buried far beneath screams;
your decay is faster than your planted seeds can grow.
The forest understands, it welcomes you into its
sticky earth,
and you may have rested in peace, if there was peace
left in the world.
You will float along the forest's edge, fed by magic
and hope,
beckoning, calling, whispering to passersby,
until the glow of the papers are buried in cement.
Until there are no longer choices to be made,
nor people left to make them.
(You were not the last to attempt to save the forest -
stanza 4)

Hope is but a speck in the sea of power,
floating at the mercy of those with control.
And indifference, though easy in action,
never rests in an equally easy end.
Such is the illusion of choice for the human,
who is but a stone that may skip--
skip-- skip again-- atop the water
only to eventually sink.

cloud

like sheets of vapor expanding with the breeze
pushed apart, to grow
to curl at the edges, to separate
to dissipate, and be born anew
the same particles of gas
the same milky white, to be seen
and forever untouched

nothing is
and always will be

I feel everything until I feel nothing
I feel everything while feeling nothing at all

UNTITLED

19

If Men come from Mars and Women from Venus,
who are those of us that came from the third planet
where it only ever rains?
Where to swim was the only lesson to learn,
and to shed tears was to worship the gods
that ruled our cloudy skies?

What do they call us on Earth,
where the Men are from Mars and the Women
are made from the rib of Men, where Venus is
inhabitable and corrosive, a land of sulphuric acid?
How can Earthlings ever comprehend the third planet
where the rain is constant and destruction never lasts
long before it is washed away?

Dear Attention-Seeker,

Life does not start with perception,
nor does it end when you are unseen.
It is a brave soul that knows its place in the world
is one that is given, not won, not earned,
For it is braver to accept what is
in the many faces of what can or could be,
than to cut away at the Ugly until it is Beautiful.

The eyes that never sleep are never satisfied.
The eyes of another will not be what saves you.
The eyes of the world cannot- will not- do more than
watch.

Luna

21

It is only natural
to bear the weight of every
expectation and inspiration
rock and speck of dust
blunt and splintering collision
and remain in devoted motion
to remain afloat, glowing amidst the blackness.

SUPERNOVA

And when the end is near,
And when it's bright, it's blinding
When it pulls at your core, relentless, inevitable,
Do you wish, instead, that it were dark?

And when the end begins,
Where the beginning of it all ends,
Where it eats and eats, collapsing and coiling,
A tunnel of snakes swallowing their tails,
Do you turn your back to the celestial hum?

And the stars are miles apart,
Do you count them before they fade?

Do you see it now,

what you left behind?

do you count your blessings

before you fade?

does it tear you to pieces

when you understand

did you wish for one last look in the mirror

?

Acknowledgements

The Earth that has given and will give;
The science that creates, the language that explains,
and the energy that is neither created nor destroyed
but only changes forms to give, and give, for eternity.

My birth, my eventual death
and the passage in between that has,
and will be, marked by the disappointment
inherent to the identity I have chosen
and been given, for this lifetime.

Those that have hurt me, before I knew hurt
and after, before I knew safety
lies in distance and high ground
and that unseen scars to the heart
never seem to heal, that they wait and bleed
until fingers reach in to pry them open
Again, and Again.

My body, which recoils at every touch;
Goosebumps that tell me when I am cold,
sweat that tells me when I am hot,
my lungs that shrivel when it is time to leave,
and my knees that will press against one another
until there are bruises to prove
that I did what I could.

Whoever is left in this world, continuing

to fight and live, to learn and love
and to read what is written.
Whoever has mastered detachment,
from bleak realities and futures that lie
only centimeters beyond
reaching fingertips and inevitable ends.